MW01169324

EMPOWERING STORIES

FOR BRAVE GIRLS

Inspiring Tales of Extraordinary
Women Who Changed the World

LILY STARLYN

LILY STARLYN

TABLE OF CONTENTS

INTRODUCTION

Have you ever wondered what it takes to change the world? What qualities do heroes possess that make them stand out and inspire us all? Imagine being faced with immense challenges and still finding the strength to rise above them, making a lasting impact on the lives of others.

In this book, we will embark on a journey of discovery and inspiration as we delve into the remarkable stories of courageous women who have defied odds, shattered stereotypes, and championed causes close to their hearts. Each chapter unveils the extraordinary lives of these trailblazers, showcasing their resilience, determination, and unwavering commitment to making a difference.

From advocating for girls' education in the face of adversity to overcoming personal struggles to reach the pinnacle of success, these women exemplify the true essence of courage and empowerment. They come from diverse backgrounds and fields—from science and sports to activism and the arts— but they share a common thread of bravery and a passion for positive change.

Join us as we learn about Marie Curie, the pioneering scientist who discovered radium and polonium, breaking barriers for women in science. Explore the inspiring journey of Serena Williams, whose resilience and skill catapulted her to become one of the greatest tennis players of all time. Discover the remarkable impact of Greta Thunberg, the teenage environmental activist who sparked a global movement for climate action.

Each chapter unfolds a different narrative of courage and determination, inviting you to reflect on the qualities that define a hero and inspire us to reach beyond our limits. As we delve into these stories, let us celebrate the triumphs, honor the struggles, and draw inspiration from the indomitable spirit of these extraordinary women.

Their journeys remind us that no dream is too big, no obstacle too daunting, and that each of us has the power to create positive change in our communities and beyond. Let their stories ignite a spark within you and encourage you to stand up for what you believe in, pursue your passions, and embrace the hero within.

Get ready to be inspired, uplifted, and empowered as we embark on this captivating journey through the lives of courageous women who have left an indelible mark on history and continue to inspire us all. This book is a celebration of their resilience, their achievements, and their enduring legacy of hope and empowerment.

The Brave Girl Who Stood Up for Education

Once upon a time, in a beautiful valley nestled among the mountains of Pakistan, there lived a courageous girl named Malala Yousafzai. Malala loved going to school, learning new things, and dreaming of a bright future. But in her village, not everyone believed that girls should go to school.

One day, when Malala was just a young girl of 11 years old, something terrible happened. The Taliban, a group that did not want girls to get an education, took control of her town. They said that girls should stay home and not go to school anymore.

But Malala knew in her heart that education was important for everyone, boys and girls alike. She believed that knowledge was power, and she wanted every girl to have the chance to learn and grow.

Malala decided to speak out against the Taliban's unjust rules. She wrote a blog under a secret name, where she shared her thoughts and feelings about education and life under the Taliban's control. Even though she was afraid, Malala's words were like a beacon of hope for many people who also wanted to see change.

As Malala's courage grew, so did her voice. She started giving speeches and interviews, bravely standing up for the rights of girls to receive an education. Her message spread far and wide, inspiring people around the world.

But not everyone was happy about Malala's bravery. The Taliban saw her as a threat to their power. One fateful day, as Malala was riding the bus home from school, a gunman boarded the bus and asked for her by name. Without hesitation, he fired his gun at Malala.

Miraculously, Malala survived the attack, but she was badly injured and had to undergo surgeries and intensive medical treatment. While she recovered, people from all corners of the globe sent messages of support and solidarity to Malala and her family.

Malala's story touched the hearts of millions. She became a symbol of courage and resilience, a beacon of hope for girls everywhere who dream of an education. Malala's voice grew even stronger after her recovery, and she continued her advocacy work on a global scale.

In recognition of her unwavering dedication to education, Malala was awarded the Nobel Peace Prize, becoming the youngest-ever Nobel laureate. She used her platform to establish the Malala Fund, an organization dedicated to ensuring every girl has access to 12 years of free, quality education.

Malala Yousafzai's story teaches us that even the smallest voices can spark big changes. She showed us that bravery and determination can overcome even the toughest challenges. Malala's journey reminds us that education is a fundamental right that should be accessible to all, regardless of gender or background.

And so, Malala's story continues to inspire children like you and me to stand up for what is right and never to stop believing in the power of education.

Triumph on the Tennis Court

Once upon a time, in the sunny state of California, there lived a determined and talented girl named Serena Williams. From a very young age, Serena loved swinging her tennis racket and hitting balls back and forth with her sister, Venus. Little did she know that she would one day become one of the greatest tennis players in the world!

Serena's journey to success was not always easy. She faced many challenges along the way, but her passion for tennis and her unyielding determination kept her going.

As a young girl, Serena dreamed of winning championships and playing on the big stages. She practiced tirelessly, honing her skills and developing her powerful serve and lightning-fast footwork. But despite her talent, Serena faced obstacles that threatened to derail her dreams.

One of the biggest challenges Serena encountered was racism and discrimination in the tennis world. As an African American woman, she often faced unfair treatment and hurtful comments. But Serena refused to let negativity hold her back. Instead, she used it as motivation to prove her critics wrong.

With unwavering resolve, Serena pushed herself to excel on the court. She entered tournaments, facing opponents much older and more experienced than her. Each match was a test of her skill and determination.

Serena's breakthrough came when she won her first Grand Slam singles title at the young age of 17. This victory was just the beginning of her remarkable career. Serena continued to dominate the tennis world, winning numerous championships and setting records along the way.

But Serena's journey was not without setbacks. She faced injuries and personal challenges that tested her resilience. However, Serena never gave up. She fought through adversity with courage and grace, always believing in herself and her ability to overcome any obstacle.

As Serena's fame grew, she used her platform to advocate for equality and empowerment. She became a role model for young girls everywhere, showing them that with hard work, determination, and self-belief, anything is possible.

Today, Serena Williams is celebrated as one of the greatest athletes of all time. Her impact reaches far beyond the tennis court. She continues to inspire millions of people around the world with her story of perseverance, resilience, and unwavering passion.

Serena's journey teaches us that success is not always a straight path. It requires dedication, perseverance, and the courage to face challenges head-on. Serena's story reminds us that we can achieve extraordinary things when we believe in ourselves and never give up on our dreams.

A Beacon of Hope and Education

In the bustling city of Chicago, there once lived a remarkable woman named Michelle Obama. She wasn't always famous; she started out as a young girl with big dreams and a love for learning.

Michelle grew up in a modest home with her parents and older brother. Her parents taught her the importance of hard work and education. They encouraged her to always aim high and never give up on her goals.

As a child, Michelle was a curious and bright student. She loved reading books and was eager to learn about the world around her. Despite facing challenges, such as growing up in a neighborhood with limited opportunities, Michelle remained focused on her studies.

Her determination paid off when she earned a spot at Princeton University, one of the most prestigious colleges in America. Michelle worked hard and excelled in her studies, earning a degree in sociology. But she didn't stop there—she continued her education and went on to attend Harvard Law School, where she earned her law degree.

After graduating, Michelle dedicated her career to helping others. She worked as a lawyer, advocating for the rights of people in her community, especially those who were often overlooked or marginalized.

However, Michelle's life changed forever when she met a young lawyer named Barack Obama. They got married, and together, they embarked on a journey that would take them to the White House.

As First Lady of the United States, Michelle Obama used her platform to advocate for important causes close to her heart. She became a passionate advocate for education, launching initiatives like "Let's Move!" to promote healthy lifestyles for children and "Reach Higher," encouraging young people to pursue higher education.

Michelle also championed women's rights and empowerment. She inspired girls everywhere to dream big and believe in themselves. Michelle believed that every girl, regardless of background or circumstances, deserved a chance to succeed.

One of Michelle's most famous initiatives was the "Let Girls Learn" program, which aimed to provide education to millions of girls around the world who faced barriers to schooling. Through this program, Michelle emphasized the transformative power of education in shaping a brighter future for individuals and communities.

Beyond her advocacy work, Michelle Obama was admired for her grace, intelligence, and compassion. She showed the world that being strong and confident doesn't mean sacrificing kindness and empathy.

Today, Michelle continues to inspire people of all ages to make a difference in their communities and strive for a better world. Her story teaches us that with perseverance, passion, and a commitment to education, anything is possible.

A Voice for Our Planet

In the serene forests of Sweden, a young girl named Greta Thunberg discovered her love for nature and animals at a very early age. She would spend hours exploring the outdoors, marveling at the beauty of the natural world. But as Greta grew older, she began to notice changes happening around her—changes that worried her deeply.

Greta learned about climate change, a big problem that was affecting our planet. She read about melting ice caps, rising temperatures, and the loss of wildlife habitats. Greta felt a sense of urgency to do something to protect the Earth she loved so dearly.

One day, Greta decided to take a stand. At the age of just 15, she began skipping school on Fridays to sit outside the Swedish Parliament with a simple sign that read, "School Strike for Climate." Greta believed that if adults weren't taking enough action to combat climate change, then it was up to the younger generation to speak up and demand change.

Greta's one-person protest caught the attention of people around the world. Soon, students and activists from different countries joined her cause, staging their own school strikes and demanding urgent action on climate change.

Greta's courage and determination sparked a global movement known as "Fridays for Future," where students and young people all over the world rallied together to raise awareness about the climate crisis and call on world leaders to take meaningful steps to protect the planet.

Despite facing criticism and skepticism, Greta remained steadfast in her mission. She delivered powerful speeches at international forums, challenging world leaders to prioritize the health of our planet and future generations. Greta's unwavering dedication earned her widespread admiration and respect.

Greta's message is clear: we all have a responsibility to take care of our Earth. She believes that everyone, regardless of age, can make a difference by making small changes in their daily lives and advocating for policies that promote sustainability and environmental protection.

Today, Greta Thunberg continues to inspire millions of people to take action for the planet. She reminds us that no one is too young to make a difference and that our voices have the power to create positive change.

A Story of Empowerment and Kindness

In a vibrant American city, a young girl named Oprah Winfrey lived in a bustling neighborhood with her grandmother. Life wasn't always easy for Oprah—she encountered numerous challenges and hardships during her childhood. However, she possessed big dreams and an unwavering spirit that propelled her to extraordinary achievements.

From a young age, Oprah had a natural gift for speaking and storytelling. She loved to read and learn, finding solace and inspiration in books. Despite the difficulties she faced,

Oprah never gave up on her dreams of making a positive impact on the world.

As Oprah grew older, she discovered a passion for media and communication. She started her career as a news anchor and talk show host, captivating audiences with her warmth, authenticity, and ability to connect with people from all walks of life.

Oprah's talk show, "The Oprah Winfrey Show," became a sensation, reaching millions of viewers around the world. Through her show, Oprah shone a spotlight on important issues, from personal empowerment to social justice, and she became a trusted friend and mentor to her viewers.

But Oprah's impact went far beyond television. She used her platform to uplift and empower others, especially women and marginalized communities. Oprah believed in the power of education and personal development to transform lives.

One of Oprah's most enduring legacies is her commitment to philanthropy. She established the Oprah Winfrey Foundation, which supports educational initiatives and provides scholarships for deserving students. Oprah's generosity has helped countless individuals access opportunities for learning and growth.

Throughout her life, Oprah faced adversity with grace and resilience. She openly shared her own struggles and triumphs, inspiring others to embrace their authenticity and pursue their dreams without fear.

As a Black woman in a predominantly white and male-dominated industry, Oprah shattered barriers and redefined what success could look like. She proved that with determination, hard work, and a compassionate heart, anyone can achieve greatness and make a positive impact on the world.

Today, Oprah Winfrey is celebrated as a media mogul, philanthropist, and advocate for empowerment and education. Her story teaches us valuable lessons about the importance of kindness, resilience, and believing in ourselves.

Liberia's First Female President

In the beautiful country of Liberia, there was once a remarkable woman named Ellen Johnson Sirleaf. Ellen had big dreams and a strong desire to make a positive difference in her country. Little did she know that she would one day become Liberia's first female president and a Nobel Peace Prize laureate!

Ellen's journey to leadership was filled with challenges, but she faced them all with courage and determination. As a young girl, Ellen loved learning and excelled in her studies. She believed that education was the key to unlocking opportunities and creating positive change.

Growing up, Ellen witnessed her country facing difficult times, including political unrest and civil war. Despite these challenges, Ellen remained committed to her goal of contributing to Liberia's development and promoting peace.

Ellen's path to leadership was not a direct one. She worked hard to build her career and gain experience in various roles, including as a government official and financial expert. Along the way, she faced discrimination and obstacles because of her gender, but Ellen never gave up.

In 2005, Ellen Johnson Sirleaf made history when she was elected as the President of Liberia, becoming the first woman to lead the country. Her election was a symbol of hope and progress, not only for Liberia but for women everywhere.

As president, Ellen focused on rebuilding Liberia's economy and infrastructure, promoting education and healthcare, and advocating for women's rights. She worked tirelessly to bring stability and peace to her country after years of conflict.

Ellen's efforts did not go unnoticed. In 2011, she was awarded the Nobel Peace Prize for her work in promoting peace, democracy, and gender equality in Liberia and across Africa. Ellen's leadership and commitment to peace inspired people around the world.

Throughout her presidency and beyond, Ellen Johnson Sirleaf continued to be a role model for women and girls. She showed that with determination, resilience, and a vision for positive change, anyone can make a difference, no matter their background or circumstances.

Ellen's story teaches us valuable lessons about the importance of perseverance and leadership. She proved that women have the power to lead and bring about transformative change in their communities and beyond.

Today, Ellen Johnson Sirleaf's legacy lives on as a trailblazer and champion of peace and equality. Her story reminds us that no dream is too big, and no obstacle is too great to overcome with determination and a commitment to making the world a better place.

Surfing Against All Odds

In the sunny state of Hawaii, there lived a spirited girl named Bethany Hamilton, who was passionate about surfing. From a very young age, Bethany spent countless hours riding waves and feeling the exhilaration of gliding across the ocean.

One fateful day, when Bethany was just 13 years old, her life took an unexpected turn. While surfing with friends, a terrifying encounter with a shark left Bethany with a life-changing injury—she lost her left arm.

Many would have been devastated by such a traumatic experience, but not Bethany.

Despite the immense physical and emotional challenges, Bethany's love for surfing remained unwavering. She was determined not to let her injury define her or hold her back from doing what she loved most.

With incredible resilience and determination, Bethany embarked on a courageous journey of recovery and adaptation. Supported by her family, friends, and the surfing community, Bethany learned to navigate life with one arm. She faced each day with positivity and a fierce determination to return to the sport she cherished.

Just weeks after the shark attack, Bethany was back in the water, learning to surf again with her newfound strength and adaptability. With unwavering perseverance, she mastered new techniques to compensate for her missing arm.

Bethany's triumphant comeback captured the hearts of people around the world. Her story of resilience and determination inspired countless individuals facing their own challenges.

Despite the physical obstacles, Bethany's surfing career soared to new heights. She competed in professional surfing competitions, fearlessly taking on powerful waves alongside able-bodied athletes. Bethany's courage and tenacity earned her widespread admiration and respect within the surfing community and beyond.

Beyond her surfing accomplishments, Bethany became an advocate for positivity and perseverance. She shared her story through books, documentaries, and motivational speeches, encouraging others to never give up on their dreams.

Today, Bethany Hamilton is not just a professional surfer; she is a symbol of hope and resilience. Her journey reminds us that setbacks and obstacles can be overcome with determination, courage, and a positive attitude.

Bethany's story teaches us valuable lessons about the power of perseverance and the importance of embracing challenges as opportunities for growth. She exemplifies the spirit of never giving up on our passions and dreams, no matter what obstacles we may face.

Empowering Voices for Equality

In the lively city of Lagos, Nigeria, there lived a talented storyteller named Chimamanda Ngozi Adichie. From a young age, Chimamanda had a deep love for words and a passion for storytelling that would one day make her a celebrated author and advocate for gender equality.

Chimamanda grew up in a close-knit family that valued education and creativity. She spent hours immersed in books, captivated by the power of stories to transport her to different worlds and inspire her imagination.

As Chimamanda embarked on her writing journey, she discovered a passion for telling stories that reflected the realities and complexities of African life. She believed in the importance of diverse voices and perspectives in literature, challenging stereotypes and misconceptions about her culture and gender.

One of Chimamanda's most famous books, "Half of a Yellow Sun," tells the story of the Nigerian Civil War through the eyes of different characters. The novel received critical acclaim and introduced Chimamanda's powerful voice to a global audience.

But Chimamanda didn't just stop at writing captivating stories—she used her platform to advocate for gender equality and challenge societal norms that limited the potential of women and girls.

In her groundbreaking TED Talk titled "We Should All Be Feminists," Chimamanda eloquently spoke about the importance of gender equality and dismantling stereotypes that hold women back. Her message resonated with people worldwide, sparking conversations about feminism and empowerment.

Chimamanda's advocacy extended beyond her words; she actively worked to uplift and empower women and girls. She established a scholarship fund to support young Nigerian women in pursuing their educational dreams and reach their full potential.

Through her books, speeches, and activism, Chimamanda Ngozi Adichie became a beacon of hope for those fighting for gender equality. She inspired women and girls to embrace their voices, challenge societal norms, and strive for a more just and inclusive world.

Today, Chimamanda continues to use her voice to advocate for positive change. Her impact on literature and feminism is profound, leaving a lasting legacy that encourages us all to embrace diversity, challenge injustice, and stand up for equality.

Chimamanda's story teaches us that words have the power to change the world. She reminds us that each of us has a unique voice and story to share, and by amplifying diverse voices, we can create a more equitable and inclusive society.

A Journey of Inspiration

In the heart of America, there lived a remarkable woman whose words danced like music and touched the souls of millions. Her name was Maya Angelou, and she was a poet, author, and civil rights activist whose legacy continues to inspire generations around the world.

Maya's journey began in the segregated South, where she faced discrimination and adversity from a young age. Despite the challenges she encountered, Maya discovered solace in the power of words and storytelling.

From a young age, Maya was captivated by the rhythm and beauty of language. She devoured books and filled her mind with the wisdom of poets and writers who came before her. Maya found refuge in the pages of books, where she discovered the power of imagination and the strength to dream beyond the limitations of her circumstances.

As Maya grew older, she found her voice through poetry and literature. Her words became a beacon of hope and resilience, shining brightly in the darkness of injustice and oppression. Maya used her pen to speak out against racism, inequality, and injustice, becoming a powerful advocate for civil rights and social change.

One of Maya's most famous works, "I Know Why the Caged Bird Sings," tells the story of her childhood and coming-of-age experiences. The book resonated with readers around the world, shining a light on the struggles of African Americans and the resilience of the human spirit.

But Maya's impact extended beyond her writing. She was also a gifted speaker and storyteller, captivating audiences with her powerful performances and inspiring messages of hope and empowerment. Maya's words had a magical quality that stirred hearts and ignited imaginations.

Throughout her life, Maya Angelou faced many trials and tribulations, but she never lost sight of her purpose: to inspire others and make the world a better place. She believed in the power of love, forgiveness, and empathy to heal wounds and bridge divides.

Maya's legacy lives on through her timeless words and indomitable spirit. She continues to inspire writers, activists, and dreamers of all ages to find their voices and speak out against injustice.

Maya Angelou's journey teaches us valuable lessons about the power of resilience, courage, and compassion. She reminds us that we each have the ability to make a difference in the world, no matter how big or small our actions may seem.

Planting Hope for the Earth

In the lush landscapes of Kenya, there lived a remarkable woman named Wangari Maathai, whose love for nature and determination to make a difference transformed the world around her. Wangari was an environmentalist and a pioneer of the Green Belt Movement, which planted the seeds of hope and empowerment across her country.

Wangari grew up surrounded by the beauty of the Kenyan forests and savannahs. She loved spending time outdoors, exploring the vibrant landscapes, and marveling at the wonders of nature. But as Wangari grew older, she witnessed the devastating effects of deforestation and environmental degradation on her beloved homeland.

Determined to protect Kenya's natural heritage, Wangari took action. She believed that trees were the key to restoring and sustaining the environment. In 1977, Wangari founded the Green Belt Movement, a grassroots initiative aimed at planting trees to combat deforestation, erosion, and the depletion of natural resources.

Through the Green Belt Movement, Wangari empowered women in rural communities by teaching them the importance of environmental conservation and providing them with the tools and resources to plant trees. Wangari believed that women, who were often the caretakers of their families and communities, played a crucial role in sustainable development.

Under Wangari's leadership, the Green Belt Movement grew into a national and international phenomenon. Thousands of women joined the movement, planting trees and reclaiming degraded lands. The simple act of planting trees became a symbol of hope, resilience, and empowerment.

Wangari faced many challenges along the way, including opposition from political authorities who viewed her activism as a threat. Despite the obstacles, Wangari remained steadfast in her commitment to environmental conservation and community empowerment.

In 2004, Wangari Maathai's dedication and impact were recognized when she was awarded the Nobel Peace Prize—the first African woman to receive this prestigious honor. The Nobel Committee acknowledged Wangari's visionary leadership and her contributions to sustainable development, democracy, and peace.

Wangari Maathai's legacy continues to inspire people around the world to take action for the planet. Her story teaches us that individual actions, no matter how small, can create positive ripple effects and bring about meaningful change.

Today, the Green Belt Movement's legacy lives on through the millions of trees planted and the communities empowered to protect their natural resources. Wangari's vision of a greener, more sustainable world continues to inspire future generations to be stewards of the Earth.

A Journey to the Top of the World

In the towering mountains of Japan, there lived a courageous woman named Junko Tabei, who dared to dream of conquering the highest peak on Earth—Mount Everest. Junko's inspiring journey made history as she became the first woman to reach the summit of Mount Everest, showing the world that determination and perseverance can lead to extraordinary achievements.

Junko's love for mountains began at a young age. Growing up in Japan, she was captivated by the beauty and mystery of the natural world. Despite societal expectations and limitations placed on women, Junko never let anything deter her from pursuing her passion for climbing.

As a young woman, Junko faced challenges breaking into the male-dominated world of mountaineering. However, she remained undeterred, pushing herself to train harder and prove her capabilities.

In 1975, Junko embarked on her historic journey to Mount Everest. The climb was grueling and filled with obstacles, from treacherous terrain to harsh weather conditions. But Junko's determination and resilience carried her forward, step by step, towards her ultimate goal.

On May 16, 1975, Junko Tabei made history when she reached the summit of Mount Everest, standing proudly at 29,029 feet

(8,849 meters) above sea level. She became a trailblazer for women in mountaineering, shattering stereotypes and inspiring countless individuals to pursue their dreams fearlessly.

Junko's achievement was not just a personal triumph—it was a testament to the power of perseverance and the courage to defy expectations. Her journey paved the way for women around the world to embrace adventure and challenge societal norms.

After conquering Mount Everest, Junko continued to climb mountains and explore remote regions, sharing her passion for adventure with others. She founded the Ladies Climbing Club in Japan, providing a supportive community for women who shared her love for mountaineering.

Junko Tabei's legacy extends far beyond her mountaineering feats. She inspired generations of women and girls to believe in themselves and reach for new heights, both literally and figuratively.

Junko's story teaches us valuable lessons about courage, resilience, and the pursuit of dreams. She reminds us that no goal is too big or too daunting if we approach it with determination and perseverance.

Today, Junko Tabei's pioneering spirit lives on in the hearts of adventurers and dreamers worldwide. Her story continues to inspire individuals to embrace challenges, break barriers, and redefine what is possible.

From Hollywood Star to Inventor Extraordinaire

In the glitzy world of Hollywood, there once lived a captivating actress named Hedy Lamarr. But behind the glamorous façade, Hedy was much more than a silver screen star—she was also a brilliant inventor whose groundbreaking work laid the foundation for Wi-Fi and GPS technologies.

Hedy's story began in Austria, where she was born Hedwig Eva Maria Kiesler in 1914. From a young age, Hedy displayed a keen interest in science and technology, fueled by her insatiable curiosity and thirst for knowledge.

As a teenager, Hedy pursued a career in acting and quickly rose to fame in Europe. Her beauty and talent captivated audiences, and she soon caught the attention of Hollywood filmmakers. Hedy relocated to the United States, where she became a sought-after leading lady in films during the Golden Age of Hollywood.

But Hedy's passion for invention never waned. In her spare time, away from the glitz and glamour of movie sets, Hedy immersed herself in the world of science and technology. She was deeply troubled by the onset of World War II and the use of radio-controlled torpedoes by the enemy.

Driven by a desire to make a difference, Hedy teamed up with composer George Antheil to develop a revolutionary invention—a frequency-hopping system designed to prevent the interception of radio signals by enemy forces. This technology, inspired by the rapid changes in piano rolls, allowed torpedoes to change frequencies in synchronization with transmitting and receiving equipment, making them virtually immune to jamming.

In 1942, Hedy Lamarr and George Antheil patented their invention, which laid the groundwork for modern wireless communication technologies, including Wi-Fi and GPS. Despite facing skepticism and disbelief at the time, their pioneering work would eventually be recognized as a crucial breakthrough in the field of telecommunications.

Hedy's story is a testament to the power of creativity and innovation. She defied expectations and transcended the confines of her Hollywood persona to become a trailblazer in the male-dominated world of science and technology.

Beyond her inventions, Hedy's legacy is a reminder of the importance of pursuing one's passions and using talents for the greater good. She believed in the potential of technology to shape the future and improve lives.

Today, Hedy Lamarr's contributions to science and technology continue to inspire inventors, engineers, and innovators around the world. Her story teaches us that anyone, regardless of background or profession, can make a profound impact by thinking outside the box and daring to pursue unconventional ideas.

Soaring to New Heights

In the wide open skies of America, there once lived a fearless aviator named Amelia Earhart, whose daring spirit and passion for flight inspired the world. Amelia's journey as an aviation pioneer began with a dream to defy gravity and reach for the clouds.

From a young age, Amelia was captivated by the wonder of airplanes. She often watched in awe as pilots soared through the sky, imagining herself behind the controls, feeling the thrill of flight.

Amelia's dream took flight when she attended an air show and experienced her first airplane ride. The exhilaration of being airborne sealed her fate—she was destined to become a pilot.

In 1921, Amelia Earhart took her first flying lesson and instantly fell in love with the art of aviation. She faced many challenges in a male-dominated field but remained undeterred, determined to prove that women could excel in aviation.

Amelia's big break came in 1928 when she was invited to join a historic transatlantic flight as a passenger. This experience fueled her ambition to achieve even greater feats in aviation.

On May 20-21, 1932, Amelia Earhart made history by becoming the first woman to fly solo across the Atlantic Ocean. She piloted her plane, the "Friendship," from

Newfoundland, Canada, to Ireland—a daring journey filled with danger and uncertainty.

Amelia's solo flight across the Atlantic captured the world's attention and propelled her to international fame. She became a symbol of courage and determination, inspiring women and girls everywhere to reach for their dreams.

Amelia Earhart's passion for aviation was matched only by her commitment to breaking barriers and expanding opportunities for women in aviation. She co-founded an organization called The Ninety-Nines, which promoted women pilots and provided support and camaraderie in the male-dominated aviation industry.

Tragically, Amelia's remarkable journey was cut short when she disappeared during an attempt to fly around the world in 1937. Her disappearance remains a mystery to this day, but her legacy as a pioneer and trailblazer endures.

Amelia Earhart's story teaches us valuable lessons about courage, perseverance, and the pursuit of dreams. She proved that with determination and a pioneering spirit, anything is possible.

Today, Amelia Earhart's spirit lives on in the hearts of aviators and dreamers around the world. Her legacy continues to inspire future generations to take to the skies and reach new heights.

Triumph Over Adversity

In a small town in Tennessee, there lived a determined young girl named Wilma Rudolph, whose journey from hardship to Olympic glory inspired the world. Wilma's story is a testament to the power of resilience and the triumph of the human spirit.

Wilma was born prematurely in 1940 and faced many health challenges from an early age. At the age of four, she was diagnosed with polio, a debilitating disease that affected her ability to walk. Wilma's legs were weak and paralyzed, and doctors feared she might never walk again.

Despite the odds stacked against her, Wilma refused to give up. With unwavering determination and the support of her loving family, she underwent years of grueling physical therapy and exercises to strengthen her muscles and regain mobility.

Wilma's hard work paid off when, miraculously, she took her first steps at the age of six. She still wore leg braces for several years but gradually regained her strength and mobility through sheer determination and perseverance.

As Wilma grew older, she discovered a passion for running. She joined her high school track team and quickly excelled despite lingering physical challenges. Wilma's natural talent and relentless drive caught the attention of coaches and scouts, who saw her potential to become a world-class sprinter.

In 1960, Wilma Rudolph made history at the Rome Olympics by becoming the first American woman to win three gold medals in track and field. She dominated the sprint events, winning gold in the 100-meter, 200-meter, and 4x100-meter relay.

Wilma's remarkable achievements on the Olympic stage made her a global sensation and a symbol of perseverance and triumph over adversity. She shattered stereotypes and inspired millions of people, proving that nothing is impossible with determination and resilience.

Beyond her Olympic success, Wilma Rudolph used her platform to advocate for civil rights and empower young athletes. She believed in the power of sports to bring people together and break down barriers.

Wilma's journey teaches us valuable lessons about resilience, perseverance, and the importance of never giving up on our dreams. She showed us that setbacks can be overcome with determination and a positive mindset.

Today, Wilma Rudolph's legacy lives on as an inspiration to athletes and dreamers around the world. Her story reminds us that with courage and determination, we can achieve greatness and defy the odds.

A Journey to the Stars

In sunny California, there lived a young girl named Ellen Ochoa, whose passion for science and exploration would one day take her beyond the stars. Ellen's remarkable journey from curious child to pioneering astronaut inspires us all to dream big and reach for the skies.

Ellen's love for science and math was evident from a young age. She was a curious and bright student, always eager to learn and explore the mysteries of the universe. Ellen's parents encouraged her curiosity and supported her academic pursuits, instilling in her a strong belief that anything was possible with hard work and determination.

As Ellen grew older, she set her sights on a career in engineering and space exploration. She earned degrees in physics and electrical engineering, mastering complex concepts and acquiring the skills needed for a career at NASA.

In 1990, Ellen Ochoa achieved a historic milestone when she became the first Hispanic woman astronaut to travel to space. She soared aboard the Space Shuttle Discovery, embarking on a mission that would change her life forever.

During her time in space, Ellen conducted important scientific experiments and contributed to our understanding of the Earth and the universe. She marveled at the beauty of our planet from above, gaining a new perspective on the interconnectedness of life on Earth.

Ellen's journey did not end with her spaceflight. She continued to break barriers and inspire others as a leader at NASA. In 2013, Ellen Ochoa was appointed as the director of NASA's Johnson Space Center, becoming the first Hispanic director and the second woman to hold this prestigious position.

As the director of the Johnson Space Center, Ellen Ochoa oversaw missions and programs that pushed the boundaries of human exploration. She was a trailblazer and role model for aspiring scientists and engineers, proving that diversity and inclusion are essential to innovation and progress.

Ellen Ochoa's story teaches us valuable lessons about perseverance, resilience, and the power of diversity in shaping the future of space exploration. She shattered stereotypes and inspired generations of young women and minorities to pursue careers in STEM (science, technology, engineering, and mathematics).

Today, Ellen Ochoa's legacy continues to inspire us to reach for the stars. Her journey reminds us that with passion, dedication, and a thirst for knowledge, we can achieve our dreams and make a lasting impact on the world.

Breaking Barriers with Grace

In a vibrant community in New Jersey, there lived a talented and determined young woman named Ibtihaj Muhammad, whose passion for fencing and unyielding spirit inspired a nation. Ibtihaj made history as the first American woman to compete in the Olympics wearing a hijab—a symbol of her faith and a testament to her courage.

Ibtihaj discovered her love for fencing at a young age. She was drawn to the grace and precision of the sport, where athleticism and strategy combined to create a thrilling competition. Despite facing challenges as a minority in the fencing world, Ibtihaj refused to be discouraged.

As Ibtihaj honed her skills and excelled in competitions, she became determined to represent her country on the world stage. In 2016, her dream came true when she qualified for the U.S. Olympic fencing team and made history as the first Muslim-American woman to compete in the Olympics wearing a hijab.

Ibtihaj's journey to the Olympics was about more than just athletic achievement—it was a triumph over prejudice and stereotypes. She used her platform to challenge misconceptions about Muslim women and promote diversity and inclusion in sports.

During the Rio Olympics, Ibtihaj's presence on the fencing strip captured hearts and inspired countless individuals, especially young girls who saw themselves represented in a sport traditionally dominated by others. She proved that with determination and self-confidence, anything is possible.

Beyond her athletic accomplishments, Ibtihaj Muhammad is a role model and advocate for social change. She founded a clothing line, Louella, that offers modest and stylish clothing options for women, celebrating diversity and empowering women to embrace their identities.

Ibtihaj's impact extends far beyond the fencing strip. She uses her voice to speak out against discrimination and promote understanding and acceptance across cultural divides. Ibtihaj believes in the power of sports to bring people together and foster unity.

Ibtihaj Muhammad's story teaches us valuable lessons about resilience, perseverance, and the importance of embracing our differences. She reminds us that diversity is our strength and that representation matters in all aspects of life.

Today, Ibtihaj continues to inspire people around the world through her advocacy and achievements. Her story serves as a powerful reminder that barriers can be overcome with determination, courage, and a commitment to positive change.

A Trailblazer in Space Math

In a quiet town in West Virginia, there lived a brilliant mathematician named Katherine Johnson, whose extraordinary calculations helped launch Americans into space and break down barriers for women and African Americans in STEM fields. Katherine's story is a testament to the power of perseverance, curiosity, and the pursuit of knowledge.

Katherine's love for numbers began at an early age. She had a natural talent for mathematics and was eager to learn everything she could about the world of numbers. Despite growing up during a time of segregation and discrimination, Katherine's parents encouraged her to pursue her dreams and excel in her studies.

Katherine's journey to NASA began when she graduated from college with degrees in mathematics and French. She joined the National Advisory Committee for Aeronautics (NACA), which later became NASA, as a "human computer"—a mathematician responsible for complex calculations before the era of modern computers.

Katherine's mathematical expertise quickly caught the attention of NASA's engineers and scientists. She was assigned to the Space Task Group, where she calculated trajectories, launch windows, and flight paths for historic space missions, including

Alan Shepard's first human spaceflight and John Glenn's orbital mission around Earth.

One of Katherine's most significant contributions was her work on the calculations for the Apollo 11 mission—the first manned moon landing. Her precise calculations were critical to the success of the mission and ensured the safe return of the astronauts to Earth.

Despite facing discrimination and segregation at work, Katherine remained focused on her passion for mathematics and space exploration. She broke down barriers for women and African Americans, paving the way for future generations of scientists and engineers.

In 2015, Katherine Johnson's remarkable achievements were celebrated in the movie "Hidden Figures," which brought her story to a global audience. The film highlighted Katherine's invaluable contributions to early space exploration and underscored the importance of diversity and inclusion in STEM fields.

Katherine Johnson's story is a source of inspiration for aspiring scientists and mathematicians everywhere. She showed us that with determination, hard work, and a love for learning, anything is possible.

Breaking Barriers at NASA

In the bustling city of Hampton, Virginia, there lived a brilliant mathematician and engineer named Mary Jackson, whose determination and passion for science helped pave the way for women and African Americans in the field of STEM (science, technology, engineering, and mathematics). Mary's story is one of courage, perseverance, and the relentless pursuit of dreams.

Mary's fascination with science and mathematics began at a young age. She excelled in her studies and developed a keen interest in understanding how things worked. Despite facing racial segregation and discrimination, Mary remained determined to pursue a career in engineering.

After graduating from high school, Mary Jackson attended Hampton Institute (now Hampton University) and earned degrees in mathematics and physical science. She began her career as a teacher but soon discovered her true calling in aerospace engineering.

In 1951, Mary Jackson joined the National Advisory Committee for Aeronautics (NACA), which later became NASA, as a research mathematician. She quickly proved her talents and was promoted to become NASA's first female African American engineer.

Mary's groundbreaking work focused on aerodynamics and airflow analysis. She conducted critical research that contributed to the design of airplanes and spacecraft, including the pioneering Mercury, Gemini, and Apollo missions.

Despite the challenges of working in a male-dominated and racially segregated environment, Mary Jackson's determination and professionalism earned her the respect of her colleagues and paved the way for future generations of women and minorities in STEM fields.

Mary's most significant achievement was her advocacy for equal opportunities within NASA. She challenged discriminatory practices and fought for the inclusion of women and African Americans in engineering and leadership roles.

Mary's contributions to NASA and her advocacy for diversity and inclusion were recognized and celebrated. In 2019, she was posthumously awarded the Congressional Gold Medal for her pioneering work and dedication to advancing civil rights and opportunities in STEM.

Mary Jackson's story is a testament to the power of perseverance and the importance of breaking down barriers. She showed us that with determination and courage, individuals can make a lasting impact on society and inspire positive change.

Today, Mary Jackson's legacy lives on as a trailblazer and role model for aspiring engineers and scientists. Her story reminds us of the importance of diversity, inclusion, and equity in STEM fields and underscores the impact of individuals who dare to dream and challenge the status quo.

Reaching for the Stars

In the bustling city of Chicago, Illinois, there lived a determined and adventurous young girl named Mae C. Jemison. Her dream of exploring the stars led her to become the first African American woman astronaut. Mae's inspiring journey to space is a testament to the power of ambition, perseverance, and a love for discovery.

Mae's fascination with space began at an early age. She was captivated by the night sky and dreamed of one day traveling among the stars. Mae's parents encouraged her curiosity and nurtured her passion for science and exploration.

Mae excelled in school, particularly in mathematics and science. She pursued her interests in college, earning degrees in chemical engineering and African and African American studies. Mae's thirst for knowledge and determination to make a difference led her to pursue a career in medicine.

After earning her medical degree, Mae worked as a general practitioner and later as a medical officer in the Peace Corps. But Mae's dream of space exploration never faded. Inspired by the achievements of other astronauts, she applied to NASA's astronaut program.

In 1987, Mae C. Jemison made history when she was selected to join NASA's astronaut corps. She became the first African American woman to travel to space, soaring aboard the Space Shuttle Endeavour on mission STS-47 in September 1992.

During her eight-day mission, Mae conducted scientific experiments focused on life sciences and conducted observations of Earth from space. She inspired millions of people around the world and proved that diversity and inclusion are essential in space exploration.

Mae C. Jemison's journey to space was about more than just breaking barriers—it was about advancing knowledge and inspiring future generations. She believed in the importance of encouraging young people, especially girls and minorities, to pursue careers in STEM (science, technology, engineering, and mathematics).

After leaving NASA, Mae continued to advocate for science education and diversity in STEM fields. She founded educational programs and initiatives aimed at inspiring young people to explore the wonders of science and pursue their dreams.

Mae's impact extends far beyond her achievements as an astronaut. She is a role model and mentor to aspiring scientists and explorers, reminding us that anyone can reach for the stars with determination and dedication.

Standing Up for Farm Workers and Civil Rights

In the sunny fields of California, there lived a courageous and compassionate woman named Dolores Huerta, whose dedication to justice and equality changed the lives of farm workers across the country. Dolores's inspiring story is one of empowerment, leadership, and the fight for dignity and rights.

Dolores grew up in a community where many families worked as farm laborers, enduring long hours, low wages, and harsh conditions. As a young girl, Dolores witnessed the struggles and injustices faced by farm workers and their families. These experiences ignited a fire within her to advocate for change.

Dolores began her journey as a community organizer, working alongside farm workers and their families to address issues of poverty, discrimination, and mistreatment. She believed that everyone deserved fair wages, safe working conditions, and respect for their contributions.

In 1962, Dolores Huerta co-founded the National Farm Workers Association (NFWA), which later became the United Farm Workers (UFW) union. Together with Cesar Chavez, Dolores led a movement to empower farm workers and demand better treatment and rights.

One of Dolores's most significant achievements was organizing the successful Delano Grape Strike in 1965. Thousands of farm workers walked off the fields to protest unfair labor practices and demand higher wages and better working conditions. The strike gained national attention and support, leading to improvements in farm workers' rights.

Dolores Huerta's leadership and activism extended beyond labor rights to civil rights and social justice. She fought against discrimination and inequality, advocating for women's rights, immigrants' rights, and access to education and healthcare for all.

Despite facing opposition and threats, Dolores remained steadfast in her commitment to nonviolent resistance and grassroots organizing. She inspired farm workers and activists to stand up for their rights and amplify their voices.

Dolores Huerta's legacy as a trailblazer and advocate for social change continues to inspire generations of activists and leaders. Her story teaches us valuable lessons about the power of collective action, perseverance, and standing up for what is right.

Today, Dolores Huerta is recognized as a fearless champion of labor rights and civil rights. She has received numerous awards and honors for her contributions to social justice and continues to inspire people around the world to fight for equality and dignity.

A Journey of Resilience and Artistry

In the colorful and vibrant world of Mexico, there lived a remarkable artist named Frida Kahlo, whose captivating paintings and indomitable spirit continue to inspire people around the globe. Frida's story is one of resilience, creativity, and the power of art to heal and empower.

Frida Kahlo was born in 1907 in Coyoacán, Mexico City. From a young age, she was drawn to art, often spending hours sketching and painting. Frida's unique style and powerful imagery would later make her one of the most celebrated artists of the 20th century.

When Frida was a teenager, she experienced a life-changing event—a tragic bus accident that left her with serious injuries, including a broken spine and pelvis. During her long recovery, Frida turned to painting as a form of therapy and self-expression.

Frida's paintings are known for their vivid colors, surreal imagery, and deeply personal themes. She often painted self-portraits that reflected her inner emotions and struggles. Through her art, Frida explored themes of identity, pain, and the complexities of the human experience.

One of Frida Kahlo's most famous paintings is "The Two Fridas," which depicts two versions of herself—one in traditional

Mexican attire and the other in a Victorian dress—symbolizing her dual heritage and identity. This painting captures Frida's deep introspection and the complexities of her identity.

Despite enduring chronic pain and health issues throughout her life, Frida Kahlo's resilience and determination never wavered. She used her art as a form of activism, advocating for women's rights, indigenous rights, and social justice.

Frida's unique style and powerful message resonated with audiences around the world. Her paintings continue to inspire generations of artists and activists, celebrating individuality and embracing imperfections.

Beyond her art, Frida Kahlo's personal life and relationships were also deeply influential. She was married to the celebrated Mexican muralist Diego Rivera, and their relationship often inspired Frida's paintings.

Frida Kahlo's legacy extends far beyond the art world. She is remembered as an icon of resilience and strength, a trailblazer who fearlessly expressed her truth through her paintings.

Today, Frida Kahlo's paintings are celebrated in museums and galleries worldwide. Her story teaches us valuable lessons about the power of creativity, resilience, and the importance of embracing our true selves.

A Brave Step Towards Equality

In the southern city of New Orleans, Louisiana, there lived a courageous young girl named Ruby Bridges, whose bravery and determination helped pave the way for equality and integration in America. Ruby's story is one of courage, resilience, and the power of one individual to inspire change.

Ruby was born in 1954 during a time of segregation when schools in the southern United States were strictly divided by race. Many African American children were denied access to quality education simply because of the color of their skin.

In 1960, Ruby Bridges made history when she became the first African American child to attend an all-white elementary school in the South. Ruby was just six years old when she took this courageous step towards integration.

Ruby's journey to school each day was a challenging one. She faced angry mobs of protesters who shouted hurtful words and held signs with hateful messages. Despite the hostility and threats, Ruby remained determined to receive an education and make a difference.

Each day, Ruby was escorted to school by federal marshals for her safety. Inside the school, she was the only African American student in her class. Despite feeling isolated and facing discrimination, Ruby showed remarkable strength and resilience.

Ruby's bravery captured the attention of the nation and became a symbol of the civil rights movement. Her story inspired people of all backgrounds to stand up against injustice and advocate for equality.

Despite the challenges she faced, Ruby Bridges remained focused on her education and the importance of breaking down racial barriers. She excelled academically and became an advocate for civil rights and social justice.

Ruby Bridges's courage and determination paved the way for future generations of students to receive equal access to education. Her story is a reminder that change begins with individuals who are willing to stand up for what is right, even in the face of adversity.

Today, Ruby Bridges is recognized as a civil rights icon and a symbol of hope and resilience. She continues to inspire young people around the world to embrace diversity, stand up against injustice, and work towards a more inclusive society.

Ruby Bridges's journey teaches us valuable lessons about the importance of empathy, courage, and perseverance in the pursuit of equality. Her story reminds us that no one is too young to make a difference and that every voice matters in the fight for justice.

A Champion of Equality and Justice

In the bustling city of Brooklyn, New York, there lived a remarkable woman named Ruth Bader Ginsburg, whose lifelong dedication to equality and justice transformed the lives of women and minorities across America. Ruth's story is one of perseverance, passion, and the relentless pursuit of equality under the law.

Ruth Bader Ginsburg was born in 1933, during a time when opportunities for women were limited. Despite facing challenges, Ruth excelled academically and graduated at the top of her class from Columbia Law School.

She was one of the few women in her law school, but she refused to be discouraged by the gender barriers she encountered.

As a young lawyer, Ruth experienced discrimination firsthand. Law firms refused to hire her because she was a woman despite her impressive qualifications. Determined to challenge injustice, Ruth began her legal career advocating for gender equality and women's rights.

In 1972, Ruth Bader Ginsburg co-founded the Women's Rights Project at the American Civil Liberties Union (ACLU). Through strategic legal cases and landmark rulings, Ruth fought to dismantle laws that discriminated based on gender.

Ruth's most significant victories came before the U.S. Supreme Court, where she argued cases that challenged discriminatory practices. Her advocacy led to groundbreaking decisions that affirmed women's rights to equal treatment under the law.

In 1993, Ruth Bader Ginsburg made history when she was appointed to the U.S. Supreme Court by President Bill Clinton. She became the second woman to serve on the nation's highest court, where she continued her lifelong commitment to justice and equality.

As a Supreme Court Justice, Ruth Bader Ginsburg earned a reputation for her sharp legal mind, meticulous approach to cases, and unwavering dedication to upholding constitutional rights. She wrote powerful dissenting opinions that inspired generations and laid the groundwork for future progress.

Ruth Bader Ginsburg's legacy extends beyond her legal achievements. She inspired millions of people, especially young women, to pursue careers in law and public service. Ruth's iconic collars and powerful words became symbols of resistance and resilience.

Throughout her life, Ruth Bader Ginsburg faced numerous health challenges but continued to work tirelessly to uphold the principles of justice and equality. She believed in the power of the law to create positive change and ensure a more just society for all.

Ruth Bader Ginsburg's story teaches us valuable lessons about the importance of perseverance, integrity, and standing up for what is right. She showed us that one person can make a difference and that progress requires dedication and determination.

Discovering the World of Chimpanzees

In the lush forests of Tanzania, Africa, there lived a young woman named Jane Goodall, whose love for animals and determination to understand them led to groundbreaking discoveries about chimpanzees and transformed our understanding of the natural world. Jane's story is one of curiosity, empathy, and the power of observation.

Jane Goodall was born in London, England, in 1934. From a young age, Jane was fascinated by animals and dreamed of living among them in the wild. Her passion for nature and wildlife sparked a lifelong adventure that would change the course of scientific history.

In 1960, at the age of 26, Jane embarked on a remarkable journey to Gombe Stream National Park in Tanzania to study chimpanzees. Armed with patience, determination, and a pair of binoculars, Jane immersed herself in the forest, observing chimpanzees in their natural habitat.

Jane's approach to studying chimpanzees was revolutionary. Instead of imposing herself on the chimpanzees, Jane patiently observed them from a distance, allowing them to become accustomed to her presence. Over time, she gained their trust and witnessed remarkable behaviors and social interactions.

One of Jane's most groundbreaking discoveries was observing chimpanzees using tools—a behavior previously believed to be unique to humans. Her observations challenged traditional views of animal intelligence and sparked new questions about the similarities between humans and chimpanzees.

Jane Goodall's research transformed our understanding of chimpanzees and reshaped the field of primatology. She discovered that chimpanzees have complex social structures, emotions, and personalities similar to humans.

In addition to her scientific discoveries, Jane Goodall became an advocate for wildlife conservation and environmental stewardship. She founded the Jane Goodall Institute to protect chimpanzees and their habitats and empower local communities to become stewards of the natural world.

Jane's work has inspired generations of scientists, conservationists, and animal lovers around the world. Her passion for protecting wildlife and promoting environmental education continues to make a lasting impact on conservation efforts.

Today, Jane Goodall is recognized as one of the world's leading primatologists and conservationists. She has received numerous awards and honors for her contributions to science and wildlife conservation.

Jane Goodall's story teaches us valuable lessons about the importance of curiosity, empathy, and respect for nature. She showed us that by observing and understanding animals, we can deepen our connection to the natural world and inspire positive change.

So, the next time you explore nature or observe animals in your backyard, remember Jane Goodall's incredible journey. Let her curiosity and passion inspire you to appreciate the wonders of wildlife, protect our planet, and make a difference in the world, just like she did.

A Hero in Disguise

In the early days of America's fight for independence, there was a brave and determined woman named Deborah Sampson, whose courage and perseverance led her to disguise herself as a man and fight in the Continental Army. Deborah's story is one of bravery, patriotism, and breaking barriers.

Deborah Sampson was born in 1760 in Massachusetts during a time when women's roles were limited. From a young age, Deborah longed for adventure and independence, but societal expectations dictated that women should stay at home and tend to domestic duties.

As tensions rose between the American colonies and Great Britain, Deborah's patriotic spirit burned bright. In 1782, at the age of 21, she made a bold decision—to enlist in the Continental Army under the alias "Robert Shirtliff."

Disguised as a man, Deborah embarked on a daring journey to fight for her country's freedom. She endured grueling training, learned military skills, and proved herself as a capable and dedicated soldier.

Deborah's true identity remained a secret throughout her service. She fought in several battles and skirmishes, demonstrating courage and determination on the battlefield. During one intense battle, Deborah was wounded by enemy fire but refused to reveal her secret.

After serving for over a year and a half, Deborah's true identity was finally revealed when she fell ill and was treated by a doctor who discovered her secret. Despite facing scrutiny and disbelief, Deborah's bravery and patriotism earned her respect and admiration.

Deborah Sampson's service in the Continental Army was unprecedented. She was one of the few women to serve disguised as a man during the Revolutionary War, challenging societal norms and proving that women were capable of fighting alongside men.

After the war, Deborah faced challenges but continued to advocate for equality and women's rights. She became one of the first women to petition the government for a military pension, advocating for recognition of her service and the rights of female veterans.

Deborah Sampson's legacy as a trailblazer and patriot continues to inspire generations of Americans. Her story teaches us valuable lessons about courage, perseverance, and the importance of fighting for equality and justice.

Today, Deborah Sampson is remembered as a revolutionary woman who defied expectations and made history. Her bravery and determination paved the way for future generations of women in the military and inspired women to pursue their dreams without limitations.

CONCLUSION

As we come to the end of this inspiring journey through the lives of remarkable women, let us reflect on the lessons learned and the impact of their courageous actions. Each story shared in this book is a testament to the power of determination, resilience, and the unwavering pursuit of one's dreams.

From Malala Yousafzai's unwavering advocacy for girls' education to Mae C. Jemison's trailblazing journey to become the first African American woman in space, these women have shown us that greatness is not defined by gender, background, or circumstance, but by the strength of character and the willingness to stand up for what is right.

Their stories have illuminated the path for future generations, inspiring young girls and boys alike to believe in themselves, embrace their passions, and work towards creating a more equitable and inclusive world.

As we celebrate the achievements of these extraordinary women, let us also recognize the importance of perseverance in the face of adversity and the impact of collective action in driving positive change.

May the stories shared within these pages serve as a reminder that every individual has the capacity to make a difference, no matter how big or small. Whether it's advocating for social justice, protecting our planet, or breaking down barriers, each of us has a role to play in shaping a brighter future.

Let us carry forward the spirit of empowerment and resilience exemplified by these women, channeling their courage and determination into our own endeavors. Together, we can continue their legacy of progress and inspire the next generation of leaders, innovators, and changemakers.

As we bid farewell to these inspiring tales, may we be inspired to embrace our own journeys with courage, compassion, and a steadfast commitment to making a positive impact on the world around us.

Thank you for joining us on this transformative exploration of courage and empowerment. May you carry the lessons learned from these incredible women as you navigate your own path and strive to leave a lasting legacy of hope and inspiration.

Made in the USA
Columbia, SC
07 June 2025

59067274R00063